THE
ĦAL SAFLIENI HYPOGEUM
Paola

ANTHONY PACE

PHOTOGRAPHY
DANIEL CILIA

HERITAGE BOOKS
IN ASSOCIATION WITH

H Heritage Malta
2004

HOW TO GET TO THE ĦAL SAFLIENI HYPOGEUM

It is recommended to pre-book your ticket as only a restricted number of visitors are allowed everyday. Reservations may be made from the Visitors Centre at the Hypogeum or from the National Museum of Archaeology.

By bus:
Bus Nos. 1, 2, 3, 4, 6, 8, 11, 12,13, 15, 17, 18, 19, 20, 21, 26, 27, 28, 29, 30 and 115 from Valletta bus terminus stopping at Paola main square. Follow the road signs to the Hypogeum.

By car:
Main roads leading to Paola and Tarxien. The easiest approach is through Vjal Santa Luċija (next to the Addolorata Cemetry). At the roundabout turn first left into Tarxien then midleft on Triq Palma, left again on Triq Ħal Saflieni and left again on Triq iċ-Ċimiterju

Insight Heritage Guides Series No: 3
General Editor: Louis J. Scerri

Published by Heritage Books, a subsidiary of Midsea Books Ltd, Carmelites Street, Sta Venera HMR 11, Malta
sales@midseabooks.com

Insight Heritage Guides is a series of books intended to give an insight into aspects and sites of Malta's rich heritage, culture and traditions.

Produced by Mizzi Design & Graphic Services

The publisher and the author would like to thank Mr Joseph Farrugia and all the staff at the site for their support.

Editorial © Heritage Books
Literary © Anthony Pace
Photography © Daniel Cilia

First published 2004

ISBN: 99932-39-93-3

THE HAL SAFLIENI HYPOGEUM

At first, it seemed that yet another early Christian catacomb had been discovered. For, indeed, the Hal Saflieni Hypogeum is not unlike the underground cemeteries of the early Christian era. It was only after the interior of the underground structure was examined that the unusual character of the monument's features was noticed. As weeks passed, it soon became clear that the Hal Saflieni discovery was much older than at first thought. The year was 1902. A century later, the Hypogeum became a centrepiece of Maltese cultural heritage and a recognized milestone in the history of world architecture. Its place among UNESCO's long list of World Heritage Sites remains undisputed.

THE DISCOVERY

In 1902, the year in which the Ħal Saflieni Hypogeum was discovered, the outskirts of Raħal Ġdid, or Casal Paola, were being transformed by new housing projects. The town was rapidly growing as a result of the steady arrival of labourers into the area, attracted by the prospect of employment at the expanding military naval docks. The landscape of the area, once characterized by patterns of field systems and snaking rubble walls, was soon covered by streets and rows of houses. Building development had in fact commenced towards the end of the nineteenth century. The Victorian street grid system is still visible today.

The development was far too advanced by the time government authorities were informed of the discovery of the Hypogeum. The site was first inspected by Dr A.A. Caruana, Malta's chief librarian and leading antiquarian, and a well-known figure in nineteenth-century cultural circles. Caruana ascertained that the discoveries were in fact man-made and were significant enough to merit protection.

A series of carefully-built foundation walls and arches to support the Victorian terraced houses, suggests that construction over the Hypogeum and its surroundings may have started years before. As a building site, Ħal Saflieni area was

Opposite: **One of the wells which lead to the discovery of the underground chambers**

Below: **The road excavations in 1902**

Bottom: **The foundations of the houses built on the Hypogeum**

placename for the area, *Tal-Għerien* ('of the caves'), suggests that the district may have been well known for cave formations and other underground features. A number of large hollows and cavities that characterize the Upper Level of the Hypogeum, stood in the way of the house-builders. These cavities had to be bridged, if allotted house plots were to be used at all. In a number of places, support walls were constructed to secure cave ceilings. Some of these walls can still be seen within the caverns that lie to the side of the main floor space of the Upper Level. Also visible are a set of foundation arches built to bridge over a wide gap located above the entrance to the Middle Level. The cutting of a number of bell-shaped wells suggests that the new house owners had also penetrated beyond the Upper Level. Visitors can still see examples of these wells in the central reaches of the Middle Level. The care with which supporting arches and foundation walls had

been constructed, and the crafting of the wells, shows how well planned the housing development had been. Sadly, the discovery of the Hypogeum will be remembered as one of the best-kept secrets of the twentieth century.

The discovery of the Hypogeum marked a new chapter in Maltese archaeological studies. Shortly after the underground cemetery was first inspected, its true antiquity began to attract scholarly attention. Maltese prehistory soon became an important area of academic interest. Pioneering syntheses of world prehistory devoted special sections to Malta's unique prehistoric antiquities. In particular, the unique qualities of the Hypogeum were given special attention. In addition, the discovery of the monument highlighted the need for an improved care of Malta's antiquities. In 1903, a few months after the discovery, a Museum Department was established under the management of a Museum Management Committee. The

A site map of the Lower Level and section drawings of the Middle Lower Levels drawn by Nicola Vassallo, in October 1907

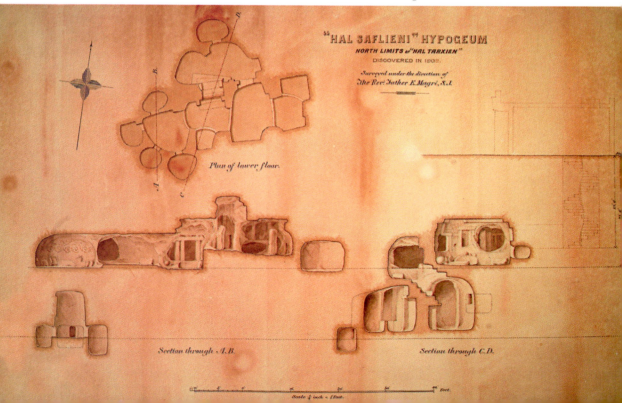

committee and the new department were also entrusted with the overall care of monuments and sites.

In November 1903, the Museum Committee of Management asked Fr. Emanuel Magri, SJ to excavate and report on the underground remains. Magri had by then established himself as one of Malta's leading scholars of the archipelago's past. In particular, he had a keen interest in antiquities, having himself accomplished a number of excavations in Malta and Gozo. The Museum Annual Report for 1906 indicates that Magri's work had been completed and the site surveyed up to the areas that had by then been acquired by government. In fact, Magri could only access the Middle and Lower Levels. The Upper Level could only be excavated later, following the purchase of the area by the authorities. In the meantime, Magri was called away from Malta on temporary missionary work in Sfax, where he suddenly passed away. Although it had been intended to publish a full report of his work at the Hypogeum, Magri's excavation records or reports have not been found.

Almost immediately, the potential of the Hypogeum as a tourist attraction was seized upon. In January 1908, the cleared chambers of the Middle Level were opened to the public. Substantial archaeological deposits still remained in the area of the original entrance (the Upper Level) which had not been accessible to Magri who only excavated the Middle Level. Later, these circumstances would throw important light on the dating of the different levels of the monument.

It was left up to Sir Themistocles Zammit, the father of Maltese archaeology, to conclude the

FR MANWEL P. MAGRI, SJ

As a foremost scholars of Malta's antiquities, Fr Manwel P. Magri, SJ was asked to form part of the first management committee of Malta's first museum. Magri was educated very much within a Jesuit framework, training at the Jesuit College and the University of Malta. At 20, Magri abandoned a prospective legal career for a religious calling. His academic training included a sound preparation in languages, philosophy, theology, and science. Throughout his career, Magri wrote extensively on Maltese traditions, folklore, history, and archaeology. In the field of archaeology, Magri covered such aspects as Phoenician inscriptions and megalithic ruins. Following the discovery of the Hypogeum in 1902, he was asked to supervise the excavation of the monument. Over-lying the subterranean monument there was then an extensive building site, with a street system being laid out to a grid pattern, servicing a series of houses. By 1903, only the Upper Level was still the property of private owners. The authorities thus had legal access only to the Middle and Lower Levels of the site. In fact Magri was able to work well within these levels, with a plan of the explored areas being made in 1906. Unfortunately, Magri was called away to Sfax, in Tunisia, on missionary duties where he passed away quite unexpectedly in 1907. The loss was a tremendous one for Malta. Magri had still to publish a report on his findings, but no draft texts have as yet come to light.

SIR THEMISTOCLES ZAMMIT

Revered as the father of Maltese archaeology, Sir Themistocles Zammit was indeed an 'all rounder' marking several achievements in a number of different fields. In the field of medicine, Zammit pursued a brilliant career as a medical practitioner, university professor, and senior government analyst in the Department of Health. These positions culminated in Zammit's milestone discovery in the summer of 1905 which explained how undulant fever (Malta fever) was transmitted. In 1920, Zammit left the medical field to take up the position of rector at the University of Malta. Throughout this period, he laid the foundations of Maltese museology and archaeology, making impressive achievements in these sectors. Zammit established the first museum of archaeology and pursued an extensive career exploring the Maltese landscape apart from undertaking three decades of excavation projects. Zammit's pioneering work in landscape archaeology focused on the renowned cart-ruts. His excavations included work at the Hal Saflieni Hypogeum, the Tarxien Temples, Ta' Hagrat, the Ghajn Tuffieha Roman Baths as well as numerous Phoenician-Punic tombs. Zammit, was the first to provide a sound framework for the chronology of Maltese antiquities. Zammit will be remembered for his epoch-making excavations of the Tarxien Temples in which the wonders of Malta's megalithic architecture and art were placed on the international map on a scale that had hitherto been unknown. From this site comes Zammit's work on the Bronze Age. Zammit became very attached to the study of Maltese antiquities and, in 1926, he resigned as university rector to dedicate more time to archaeology. Zammit was a prolific writer, publishing important works in the field of archaeology, education, literature, medicine, public health, and Maltese history. Zammit passed away in 1935, at the age of 71.

excavations at Ħal Saflieni. It was immediately evident that the monument was an important scientific discovery that was bound to attract international attention. The Upper Level provided Zammit with significant insights on the sequence of the site's prehistory, the ritual spaces of the monument, some of the site's external features, and the estimated number of individuals who may have originally been buried in the site. Zammit noted that intact deposits survived only in the Upper Level. A substantial part of one of these deposits has been preserved and can still be seen in a large chamber situated to the left of the Upper Level's main axis. Zammit also noted a number of hollows, possibly tombs, as well as a number of megaliths in areas beneath the modern street surface. Zammit

A contemporary photo by R. Ellis of the Hypogeum shortly after its discovery

was only able to photograph these remains.

The monument was mapped anew in 1952 as part of a general survey of Malta's prehistoric antiquities. This exercise also included surveying of the Hypogeum's ochre paintings that decorate the main chambers of the Middle Level. The objects and pottery previously found by Magri and Zammit were also re-examined. Between 1990 and 1993, excavations were again undertaken at the site by the present author, Nathaniel Cutajar, and Reuben Grima as part of the Museums Department conservation project.

These excavations re-visited the areas that had last been seen and photographed almost a century earlier by Zammit. These most recent excavations have provided additional information concerning the original entrance area of the Hypogeum.

Unfortunately, the monument had to be closed to the public for nine years between 1991 and 2000. The pressures of tourism and the excessively high numbers of visitors began to leave a mark on its fragile environment. During this period, an extensive conservation project was designed after a number of research projects had been undertaken during previous years. The conservation arrangements aim at providing a good visitor experience, by imposing a sustainable system of controlled visitor numbers, regulating light levels and intensity, as well as a protective system of climatically-controlled buffer zones.

MALTA AND MEDITERRANEAN PREHISTORY
5200-2500 BC

The story of the Hypogeum is intimately tied to Malta's role and position in Mediterranean prehistory. The archipelago lies just over 90 km south-east of Sicily. The islands do not possess the conspicuous high grounds of Sicily. So whereas the high lands of Sicily can be made out from Malta on clear days, the islands are hardly visible from Sicily. Yet the islands may have already been known to the Neolithic farmers of the Stentinello area, near present-day Syracuse, in south-east Sicily. It was from this area that farming may have been introduced to Malta and Gozo, some time during the middle of the sixth millennium BC. Indeed, pottery of the Għar Dalam phase (5200 BC) bears a number of similarities to contemporary ceramics used in the Stentinello area.

The Maltese islands may have been attractive because of their geographic location. Being removed from Sicily, the archipelago offered the benefit of autonomous survival but with just enough resources to support small communities. Indeed, the limited land resources of the islands would probably not have been able to sustain viable hunting and gathering communities on a permanent basis. Such communities relied on the sustainable use of seasonal and migratory food sources. However rudimentary or complex, agriculture would have thus been a decisive factor in the use of the Maltese islands as a home. Were it not for the arrival of agriculture in South Italy and Sicily, the permanent occupation of the islands might have occurred in later centuries.

The short sea-crossing from Sicily could pose little danger if planned well and undertaken in optimal seafaring conditions. Small vessels would have been used to ferry people and a 'Neolithic kit' of wheat, cattle, pigs, sheep, and goats, as well as necessary materials. Initially, even a very small group of families would have been sufficient to form viable communities. These small pioneering communities were later to spawn one of the most remarkable cultures of world prehistory. The Sicily Channel may have very well acted as a filter for human interaction, but the Maltese islands were never completely isolated.

Sicily and other central Mediterranean islands were key focal points for cultural interaction and exchange. The extent, volume, and frequency of communication are not very clear. The inhabitants of the Maltese archipelago would most likely have assumed a certain degree

During prehistory, rock-cut chamber tombs first appeared in the Central Mediterranean (darker shade)

Italy

Sardinia

Sicily

Gozo

Malta

CHRONOLOGY OF MALTESE PREHISTORY
BASED ON CALIBRATED CARBON 14 DATES*

Period	Phase	Date
Early NEOLITHIC	Għar Dalam	5200 – 4500
	Grey Skorba	4500 – 4400
	Red Skorba	4400 – 4100
LATER NEOLITHIC	Żebbuġ	4100 – 3800
	Mġarr	3800 – 3600
	Ġgantija	3600 – 3000
	Saflieni	3300 – 3000
	Tarxien	3000 – 2500
BRONZE AGE	Tarxien Cemetery	2500 – 1500
	Borġ in-Nadur	1500 - ?
	Baħrija	900 – 8th century BC

Għar Dalam

Grey Skorba

Red Skorba

Żebbuġ

Mġarr

Ġgantija

Saflieni

Tarxien

Tarxien Cemetery

Borġ in-Nadur

Baħrija

* Rounded to nearest calibrated Radiocarbon dates

A 180° view of the
Middle Level showing
the Main Chamber
and the transitional
lobby space leading
to Zones B and C

of duality in their life-styles. On the one hand, the islanders would have had to maintain contacts with the outside world. Obsidian was imported from Lipari and Pantelleria. Red ochre and flint, from the Monti Iblei, would have likewise necessitated crossings to Sicily. Other stone materials would have required contacts with farther regions.

When it comes to the exchange of ideas, the archaeological evidence becomes more difficult to interpret. For instance, the emergence of underground rock-cut burials is a central Mediterranean cultural phenomenon, with Malta and Gozo being among the places where the oldest examples of this rite were performed. The phenomenon is essential for understanding the origins of the Hypogeum. Was the custom of rock-cut chamber tombs known or extensively diffused? Were the communities that practised this form of burial, linked by long-standing ties of kinship or ancient cultural roots? Common to many islands and remote places was the development of seemingly unusual phenomena. The Maltese islands appear to have gone their own way to develop a form of megalithic architecture that has so far not been linked to similar or identical buildings elsewhere. The megalithic phenomenon of the Maltese islands remains unique.

Whatever the degree of isolation, the inhabitants of Malta and Gozo were not short on developing a refined sense of living. The islanders appeared to have maintained a complex religious and ritual belief system. Their sense of science and technology appears to have been equally advanced. The islanders

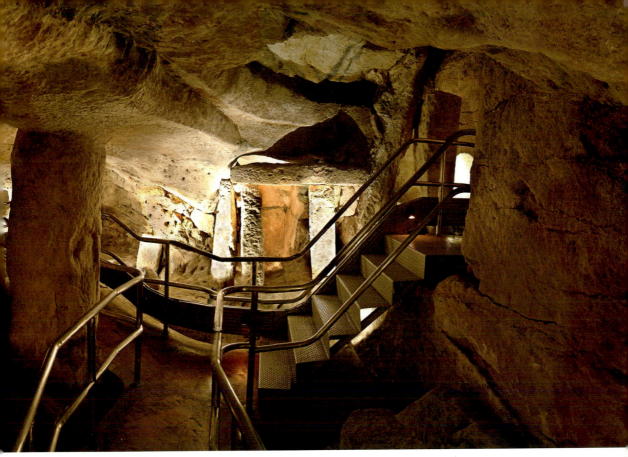

developed a unique architectural tradition, an outstanding repertoire of art works, and an equally impressive sense of scientific observation. From small huts, the islanders moved on to develop monumental architecture. Cemeteries were at first small chambers cut into the rock. Later some central burial grounds became larger and more elaborate, often mirroring surface architecture. Pottery became more refined, with forms and decorations that still capture a fresh sense of design and artistic creativity. The islands' art was remarkably well advanced, with aesthetic values that are central to the history of art. In science, the Neolithic farmers of the islands appear to have developed their own understanding of the physical world. Monuments could act equally as central places of worship or social interaction or else as calendars.

Cemeteries, monuments, art, and the development of social identity became important tools of survival and social evolution. Monuments and other physical relics became significant icons which, like present-day flags and national anthems, embodied the islanders' past, present concerns, and future aspirations. Such terms help us understand some of the many possible explanations as to why the Hypogeum developed as it did. In a world that was obviously much wider than the limitations of an island life-style, the Hypogeum may have provided a much-needed focal point, where remembrance played an important role in shaping identity.

ROCK-CUTTING TECHNIQUES

The creation of the Hypogeum's interior is awe-inspiring. The techniques employed by the prehistoric craftsmen are not far removed from those used by stonemasons and quarrymen before the advent of mechanized rock-cutting. In the case of the Hypogeum, however, the rock-cutting methods were even more remarkable considering that the Temple-Period craftsmen did not apparently possess metal tools. Collections at the National Museum of Archaeology include a number of stone hammers, chisels, chert and flint blades, as well as antler picks. Such tools provide a glimpse of rock-cutting technology, however simple it may have been.

Although the Hypogeum appears to be rather organic in comparison to the more symmetrically-built temples, the layout of the underground cemetery may have been partly influenced by the requirements of rock-cutting. The choice of the location may have been an important consideration for craftsmen. The surface levels of the Hypogeum may have been friable enough to enable quarrying. Some geological features even suggest that the upper layers of the site may have comprised a number of natural caves and fissures that may have facilitated the planning of the cemetery. Such features were, however, modified beyond their natural configuration. Whatever the case, all the levels and surroundings of the Hypogeum reflect extensive rock-cutting.

As to the rock-cutting itself, a number of techniques appear to have been used. Geological features, such as cracks or fissures, were exploited to facilitate the cutting of larger volumes of rock. A number of small holes found in various chambers within the Hypogeum suggest that rock masses were often broken by drilling and leverage techniques. Other implements, such as hammers and picks, would have facilitated work. Chert, flint, or obsidian blades may have at times been used for finer carvings. Hard stones or pebbles may have been used to achieve smooth finishes on the walls.

The completion of the Hypogeum must have required a number of years. Work would have occupied a small work force that had to be organized into gangs that alternated between quarrying, stone dressing, and removing debris. Skilled craftsmen would have created the architectural replicas as well as the spiral paintings.

PREHISTORIC DEATH CULTS AND CEMETERIES

The few cemeteries known from Maltese prehistory suggest that the Ħal Saflieni Hypogeum was the result of a long period of development and changes that characterized much of what occurred in various different places in the archipelago. The available archaeological evidence suggests a number of possible avenues of investigation. The one followed here links chronological evidence with different monument typology.

If only to simplify enormous time-scales which are now far removed in time, the following explanation will outline a three-stage development. The three-stage development first saw the introduction of the earliest rock-cut chamber tombs during the Żebbuġ Phase (4100-3800 BC). These early tombs consisted of simple chambers that were accessed through a shaft. The Ta' Trapna (Żebbuġ) burials may represent an alternative form of grave which may have consisted of rock-cut hollows. A similar burial

was unearthed at San Pawl Milqi, a site which is close to the prehistoric temple of Tal-Qadi. Żebbuġ-period tombs found at the Xagħra Circle on Gozo show that the rite of collective inhumations was already practised at such an early stage.

Collective inhumation is, by definition, characterized by the intentional burial of deceased in one tomb. Simultaneous burials may have sometimes occurred. However, it is clear that a multiple re-use of the same tomb over very long stretches of time

Evolution in rock-cutting

Nadur tomb

Xemxija tomb 3

Xemxija tombs 1 & 2

Hypogeum

Above: **Human remains from Xagħra Circle, where it is believed, primary, secondary and later burials were, in some cases, practised**

Left: **A reconstruction of a rock-cut chamber tomb of the type known from the Central Mediterranean In the Maltese islands such tombs can still be seen at Xemxija and the Xagħra Circle**

The 'crouched position' was a familiar ceremonial position to lay the dead in their final rest place. The deceased were often sprinkled with a thin layer of red ochre

The circular entrances to the Zebbug tombs at Xaghra Circle. The linear cavities and cuts are modern vine trenches

requirements. Tombs served many purposes. Primarily, they offered a formal burial ground for the deceased, but they also served as ossuaries. Primary burials would have been pushed back to make space for new ones. This repeated primary and secondary burial functions also meant that underground burial chambers served as places of remembrance. The social implications of this cultural phenomenon are now difficult to assess. In the past, scholars ascribed such practices to a form of ancestor cult, which has unfortunately remained undefined. It appears, however, that an insistence on the use of the same tombs may have had a special meaning. Collective remembrance, collective pasts, and collective responsibilities are synonymous with the various ways that humankind has devised to deal with social behaviour. 'Collective' therefore came to be defined and expressed in a number of ways. Often, special monuments have been designed to capture the idea

may have been the established custom. The rite of cut underground tombs appears to have developed first in the central Mediterranean, specifically in the South Italian regions, Sicily, and the Maltese islands. Communication between the people of these regions may have led to the spread of the idea of underground rock-cut tombs. In South Italy, rock-cut chamber tombs were also used for single inhumations. So far, it appears that the rite of collective burials may have been exclusively followed in Malta.

This practice had its special

of collectivity. Such monuments become at once, purposeful, symbolic, and iconographic. The physical development of such monuments becomes synonymous with the need to assert collective identities. The physical size of monuments therefore becomes a matter of importance. An expression of collectivity by communities and their descendants could take various forms. For instance, cemeteries comprising a number, or hundreds, of individual graves have become a common practice.

It seems that in Neolithic Malta, this expression of collectivity appears to have encouraged the expansion of the very physical spaces within established tombs. Community bonding appears to have led to the physical bonding of burial spaces. Small rock-cut chamber tombs, measuring just over a metre across, could cater for a small number of individual burials. Communal needs would have required more space. In addition, small tombs lacked a sense of the monumental, which is very often an element of remembrance. The type of small tombs used during the Żebbuġ phase may have therefore become less fashionable. Larger burial spaces may have steadily acquired more importance. If this reading of such concerns is correct, then one would expect to trace some evidence of it in the archaeological record.

A monumental trilithon was constructed to the left of the main passage way of the Upper Level. In this area, a series of chambers lead to a water cistern, cut to a depth of 8 metres (*below*)

Such evidence is to be found at various archaeological remains of the Ġgantija phase (3600-3000 BC). It was during this important phase that the second stage in the development of funerary monuments occurred. Looking at the distribution patterns of known funerary sites, it would appear that while a number of simple rock-cut chamber tombs continued to be used, a preference for larger facilities began to manifest itself. The upper level of the Ħal Saflieni Hypogeum, the use of the Xagħra Circle, Xemxija I, II, and V, as well as Bur Mgħeż cave certainly become more conspicuous in the archaeological repertoire. At the Hypogeum, the refashioning of the Upper Level followed a deliberate expansion of existing burial space. A large hollow was cut to serve as an entrance lobby to the monument. Chambers were cut on either side of the main axis of the lobby. The first faint signs of rock-cut architectural features make an appearance on this level. At

Xemxija, a similar phenomenon of ritual space enlargement took place. In particular, two tombs, Xemxija I and II, were linked by a hole cut in the rock wall that separated the two tombs. This interconnecting hole is possibly the most eloquent indication of the need for enlarged communal burial spaces. At the Xagħra Circle, the monumental aspect of the cemetery began to take shape probably around this time. Clearly, evidence from this site suggests that while the double-chambered Żebbuġ tomb continued to be used during the Ġgantija phase, more 'common' space was required.

Explanations for what now may appear to be a sudden development will remain a matter of debate. The archipelago may have experienced centuries of viable living conditions that may have in turn encouraged demographic growth. This growth may have reflected itself in a wider distribution of monuments. Even more important, this period saw the emergence of megalithic building

complexes, generally referred to as temples. The construction of so many megalithic buildings, almost in a sudden development, still begs explanations. The limited number of radiocarbon dates makes the phenomenon look even sharper than it may actually have been in reality. What seems to be missing is evidence for a longer tradition of architectural construction. The picture is distorted because of the unevenness of the evidence itself. Traditionally, Maltese archaeology has focused almost entirely on the megalithic temples whose sheer presence has towered above many other important research areas. For instance, the temples have attracted more attention than the lesser buildings of the same period. Yet the excavations from Skorba show that, as early as 5200 BC, buildings of some form were being constructed. By the Grey (4500-4400 BC) and Red Skorba Phases (4400-4100 BC), more elaborate structures were being built to host rituals or sacred activities. What happens in the Ġgantija phase is, however, different in many respects. A decision appears to have been taken to transform construction methods. Henceforth, buildings were to be built for posterity. Their materials had to be durable to withstand the test of time. Their place in the landscape was to be ensured through the use of megaliths. Their use and function was to be multi-purpose, and through the ages they were to serve as repositories of a repertoire of art objects. Cumulatively, these impressive monuments may have come to embody universal knowledge, traditions, and customs that could be transmitted from one generation to another by means of monumental architecture.

The elaboration of tomb plans during the Ġgantija Phase was paralleled by the higher distribution of cemeteries across the landscape. This phenomenon may reflect a degree of decentralized customs, at a time when megalithic architecture was first becoming more profuse throughout the archipelago. Further research may yet shed more light into the intriguing distribution patterns of the Ġgantija phase burial sites. The peak reached during this phase contrasted significantly with the distribution patterns of the previous phases and those of the following Tarxien phase.

The third and final stage in the development of burial-site typology occurred during the Tarxien Phase. This stage was again to see a second period of megalithic building with existing structures being altered, expanded, and elaborately embellished. A similar expansion took place in the central cemeteries among which were the Ħal Saflieni Hypogeum, the Xagħra Stone Circle, and Bur Mgħez. Unlike the first two sites, very little is known of Bur Mgħez, a cave which seems to have still offered a large enough space for extended communal burial rites. In the case of the Hypogeum, the cemetery was deliberately extended beyond the upper level (Ġgantija Phase) where older burials remained intact. The site was elaborately embellished with superb rock carvings and ochre paintings. A similar elaboration seems to have

Beautifully designed clay pots, having particular forms and decorations, often formed part of the votive offerings that accompanied the dead (28x42 cm)

Carinated bowls, typical of the many similar containers found at the Hypogeum (25x44 cm)

occurred at the Xagħra Stone Circle where well-crafted megaliths, a monumental entrance, and several internal ritual features were incorporated in the site. The site was enclosed by an extensive megalithic wall that has now been superseded by a modern rubble wall which, however, still defines the original confines of this cemetery.

Expansion of centralized burial sites was by no means the only phenomenon. If such a deliberate expansion had been planned to accommodate growing social demands for access rights into central ritual sites, the impact of such an ideological development would have been felt throughout the small communities of the archipelago. Such a cultural phenomenon may have left a mark on the archaeology of the Maltese islands. Indeed, it appears that throughout the Temple Period, the enlargement of central cemeteries was paralleled by the disappearance of smaller burial places. The demand for such large centralized cemeteries may have led to the disappearance of the smaller burial sites.

By the Tarxien phase (3000-2500 BC), many of the known smaller burials sites appear to have gone out of use. The table indicating the diagnostic dating pottery-types found at sites, suggests that towards the closing centuries of the Temple Period, only the large cemeteries such as Ħal Saflieni, Bur Mgħez, Xemxija, and the Xagħra

Circle were still active. This activity appears to have been complex, with a variety of rites being practised. Monumental embellishments became more pronounced. At the Xagħra Circle on Gozo, ceremonial passage-ways marked by flagstones and standing stones, were installed at strategic locations within the circle enclosure. Within the Circle itself, dressed megaliths, similar to those found within the temples of Mnajdra and Ħaġar Qim, were used to define burial spaces. The best surviving example of this complex monumentality is undoubtedly the Ħal Saflieni Hypogeum. Here, the site was meticulously carved out of the live rock. Interiors were embellished with reproductions of some of the architectural features that had already been used in the temples. Within the underground cemetery, red ochre pigment was used to colour walls and ceilings. Everywhere across the archipelago, the 'underworld' of the dead was given physical personification through a tradition of funerary architecture.

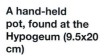

A hand-held pot, found at the Hypogeum (9.5x20 cm)

PAINTINGS FOR THE DEAD

Red was the colour of the dead. The pigment was produced from crushed ochre, a clay containing red iron oxides whose source has eluded scholars. Sicily has traditionally been identified as the most likely place from where this dark reddish earth may have been obtained. The Hypogeum is the only site in Malta where Temple-Period paintings have so far been identified.

Red pigment was used to colour statuettes or to highlight designs on pottery. Plaster, known to have possibly been used in the temples themselves, may have also been painted, partly in red. Within the Hypogeum itself, the facade in the main chamber in Zone A still retains remnants of large tracts of red pigment. Red was also associated with burial rituals. The dead were often sprinkled with red ochre in side rock-cut chamber tombs. The connotations of these customs still escape clear explanations, but the repeated use of red pigment in funerary contexts is suggestive of the significant role that colour may have played in rituals. Indeed, such significance may have been such as to warrant periodic crossing to Sicily to obtain ochre.

On the other hand, the Hypogeum paintings fall very much into a category of achievements that contrasts greatly with other aspect of Maltese prehistoric art and architecture. Whereas the art and architecture of the megalithic temples reflects a high sense of organized composition and design, the Hypogeum paintings are visibly more organic and less structured. One gets the impression that whereas the craftsmen of the Temple Period excelled in creating three-dimensional art, relief sculpture, and architectural designs, they appear to have been less successful in developing painting to similar levels of achievement. Being so far the only paintings known from the period, the Hypogeum images may be too small a sample to be a good representation of Temple-Period painting traditions.

What do the Hypogeum paintings represent? Once again, interpretations vary and many have become tinged with much unguarded speculation. The images have still to be deciphered, and till then, one must be content with admiring the structure and composition of the images for their own sake. In general, the images follow very much the idea of spirals. Within the temples, spirals were invariably rendered in a highly-structured manner. The faces of decorated megaliths appear to have been carefully measured and the spirals themselves laid out in such a way as to be well-organized in symmetrical arrangements. The spirals on temple megaliths are almost invariably very similar in terms of measurements and rendering.

In the Hypogeum, the spiral becomes very organic, in places taking on the characteristics of a straggling plant. Did the funerary context of the Hypogeum require symbols that were slightly different from those of the temples? Were the Temple-Period artists masters at three-dimensional creations and architectural designs, but poor painters? Did the restricted spaces within the Hypogeum make painting uncomfortable or technically difficult? Or did the dark interiors of the underground cemetery simply inspire a new art form in which the use of red pigment held a particular significance?

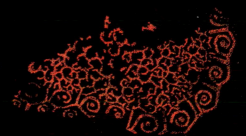

GIFTS FOR THE DEAD

The dead were buried in dark soil, accompanied by offerings of special objects. Some items found in the Hypogeum were once personal ornaments such as necklaces, pendants, and beads. In some cases, funerary offerings included beautiful artworks, such as figurines or objects that once involved many hours of refined craftsmanship. The most remarkable object was the small figure of a reclining female, better known as the 'Sleeping Lady'. The clay figurine may have been intended to be an iconographic representation of death or the afterlife. Other statues were made of local stone, but two in particular were manufactured of an alabaster-like material which was clearly imported, possibly from the Italian mainland. Imported materials may have had a special significance. Their procurement entailed risk, a crossing to Sicily, as well as possible overland journeys. Once imported, such materials or items became objects of value. The Hypogeum also yielded a collection of polished stone-axes, all shaped and finished to a high standard of craftsmanship.

The significance of such funerary customs is now lost and one can only guess that such offerings were meant to accompany the dead in the afterlife. But the burial of valuable objects also says much about society itself. Valuable objects denoted a certain degree of status that was accorded to the deceased, as well as the status of those who were left behind to bury the dead. In addition, funerary gifts also meant that prized artworks and objects of status were taken out of circulation in spite of the hard work that often went into their creation. Burial of such objects may have thus enhanced the value of, and the demand for such items, in the same way that hoarding of precious metals increased the importance of such materials. Whatever the case, the dead were provided with possessions of important significance. The beauty and refinement of such offerings were probably such as to make a social statement during ceremonies and funerary rituals.

Top: **Hypogeum Limestone heads 9x8.2 cm (*left*) and 11x7.2 cm (*right*). The headless statuette was found in a pit on the Upper Level (see page 26). Traces of red pigment appears on various parts of the body. (height 39 cm, width 27 cm, depth 16.8 cm)**

From the Hypogeum come three figures lying on a couch. The use of the couch is a common symbol which now escapes a clear understanding. The statuette above depicts a headless (decapitated?) figure (height 4 cm, length 9 cm, width 5.6 cm). The other statue, right, represents a complete figure shown in a position which is not unlike the 'counched' burial position often encountered in prehistoric cemeteries (height 7 cm, length 12 cm, width 6.8 cm).

THE ORIGINS AND DEVELOPMENT OF THE HYPOGEUM

The Hypogeum is known to date back to at least about 4000 BC, if not slightly earlier. Żebbuġ Phase pottery from this period has been discovered on site. The surface level, which now corresponds to more or less the modern street level, would most probably have been the oldest part of the monument. During later centuries, the surface areas appear to have been extensively modified by the construction of a megalithic building. A few traces of this building have been unearthed during the latest excavations. By the Ġgantija Phase (3600-3000 BC), the present-day Upper Level had also come into use. Extensive rock cutting and modifications of this level may have initially taken place around this time. The Middle and Lower Levels were finished later still, during the Tarxien Phase (3000-2500 BC). According to ^{14}C dating therefore, it would appear that the

Hypogeum was used over a span of many centuries during which the monument experienced a number of modifications as it was enlarged to accept more and more burials.

The 1990-92 excavations suggest that the Hypogeum may have once had a monumental structure built directly on top. The full extent of this building is now unknown. It is possible that a shrine once guarded a ceremonial passage into the cemetery. Early ideas of where such an entrance could have been suggested an area roughly in the north-west corner of the present building. For Zammit, basing himself on the meagre information available, a group of standing stones that can still be seen today, suggested a possible passage-way.

The 1990-92 excavations threw some light on this problem. It was clear, for example, that substantial rock-cutting had been undertaken

The monumental trilithon located on the Upper Level, viewed from the side chamber

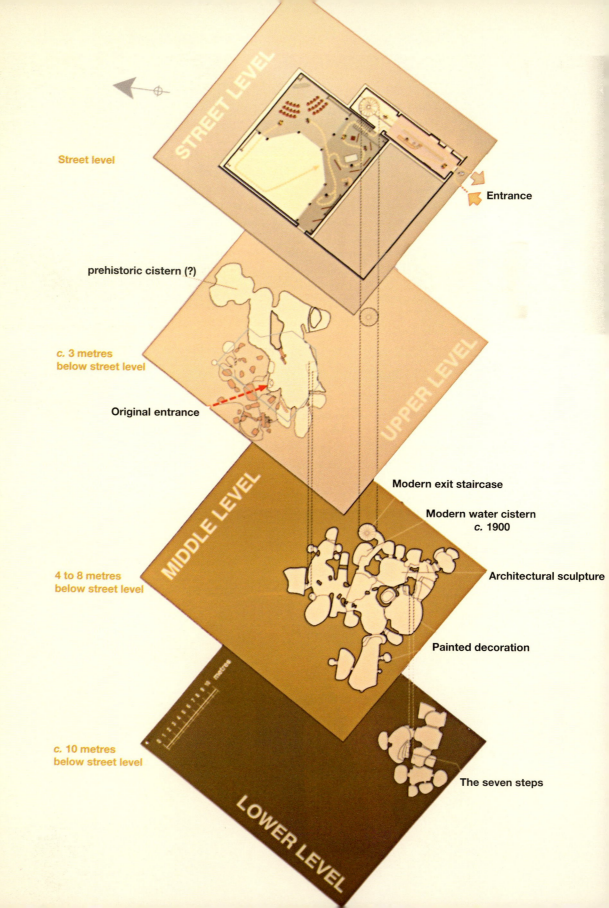

STREET LEVEL

Street level

Entrance

prehistoric cistern (?)

c. 3 metres
below street level

Original entrance

UPPER LEVEL

Modern exit staircase

Modern water cistern
c. 1900

MIDDLE LEVEL

4 to 8 metres
below street level

Architectural sculpture

Painted decoration

c. 10 metres
below street level

The seven steps

LOWER LEVEL

during prehistory. Indeed, the entire lip of the promontory was cut away, so that a rough curve now defined the profile of the entrance area. This profile can still be seen under the modern wall of the present building. Towards the mid-section of this cut-away, a passage was cut perpendicular to the curved profile. This passage is now partly covered by the modern removable walk-way. A well-shaped megalith, now hidden underneath the north wall of the modern building, served as a threshold. It seems that the huge cut-away and the passage were designed to facilitate access from the external higher ground into what is now referred to as the Upper Level. The excavations showed that this access ramp extended outwards into an area that now lies underneath the adjoining street. The main axis of the passage-way has been shown to lie roughly in a west-north-westerly direction, that is, away from the area originally identified by Zammit. Just to the south of the passage-way, a number of worked megaliths suggest that a structure once stood in this

area. The structure appears to have consisted of cut hollows, constructed walls, and chambers with porthole entrances. The function of this structure is now difficult to establish, but it is clear from these surviving ruins that the Hypogeum once extended well beyond the limits that are accessible today.

The Upper Level has survived to a great extent. The level is nothing more than a large hollow that had been quarried into the upper rock layers of the Ħal Saflieni promontory. Originally, this level had been accessed through the ramp which extends from the external areas of the monument into the main central space of the Upper Level. Once past the access ramp, prehistoric visitors would have had to walk over two strategically-located tombs. Was the position of these tombs intentional, marking some rite of passage?

Once past these tombs, visitors would have found themselves in the middle of the Upper Level which functioned as one of the monument's transitory spaces, a sort of lobby. A

To the right of the main passage way of the Upper Level lie three chambers, dating to the Ggantija phase (3600 BC)

A 'headless' standing statue and two limestone heads were discovered in this pit (see page 22)

Below: Sir Temi Zammit left a 'spoil heap' from his excavations in a chamber which lies to the right of the entrance to the Middle Level

Right: Rock-cutting, often followed natural fissures. In some chambers, tool marks can still be made out

monumental trilithon still stands to the north of the main passage. To the right and left of the main axis, a number of chambers were cut into the side-walls of the lobby space. These chambers resemble low-lying caves on account of the limited headroom they afford. The chambers are roughly-finished and lack the highly-finished embellishment of the Middle Level. The Upper Level chambers have indeed been likened to the Xemxija tombs which are, however, much smaller in dimension.

A surviving prehistoric burial deposit was left behind by Sir Temi Zammit for future generations of archaeologists to examine. This deposit, located in the first chamber to the left of the main axis, provides insights into one of the possible burial methods used in the Hypogeum. In effect, a good number of spaces and chambers of the Hypogeum contained sunken floors. In some places, hollows of many forms are also present. Today, almost all of these chambers and features of the Hypogeum are clean of soil deposits. However, this may not have been so during prehistory. Judging by the deposit left behind by Zammit, it would appear that sunken floors, hollows, and low dividing walls may have served as a system of earth repositories. Burials would have taken place in earth deposits, rather than on clean floors. In many chambers, soil marks can still be made out on walls.

The Middle Level has a different character. It was designed to be a complex space with elaborate decorations and a more extensive system of chambers and passages. The Middle Level is accessed through a small intermediate floor which serves as the transitory link with the Upper Level. A sudden drop of about a metre from this transitory floor through yet another entrance leads directly into the Middle Level. The first space encountered is roughly-finished, giving the impression that it was somehow left unfinished. This

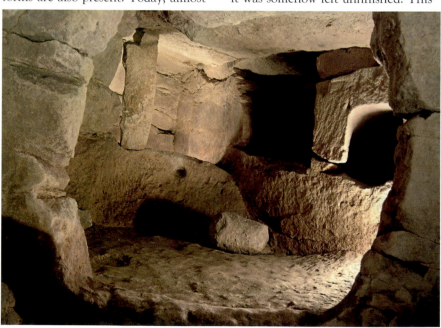

space, in fact, marks quite a contrast with the view provided by the main decorated chamber, which is immediately visible from the entrance to the Middle Level. This space is nevertheless a very important one for a number of reasons. Firstly, it appears to have functioned as the internal lobby area of the Middle Level. From this lobby, access is possible to the other areas of the level. Secondly, the area originally received the first incoming light from the external parts and the Upper Level. This internal lobby therefore doubled up as a light channel.

In reality, the level of light penetration would have varied from one area to another, on account of a number of factors. For instance, the difference in height between the Middle Level entrance and the floor of the level's interior would have influenced the angle at which light would have penetrated into the inner reaches of the monument. There is then the different angle at which the external and interior

entrances of the transitory level leading down to the Middle Level had originally been cut, an arrangement that may have served to filter light penetration. The scale of openings and their strategic positions linking interior spaces would have facilitated illumination, even if at a reduced level. The large circular hole leading into the Main Chamber enabled a higher level of light to enter this area. The carved entrance located opposite to this circular viewing point would have in turn facilitated the illumination of the inner chamber, the so-called 'Holy of Holies'. Similarly, two rectangular apertures cut into the dividing wall between the Main Chamber and the Painted Chamber, would have diverted indirect light into Zone B. Zone C, lying perpendicular to the main axis of the internal lobby space, would have had the weakest illumination.

Issues of illumination have always played an important role in the way that underground spaces and

Unique in the history of world architecture, the Hypogeum is marked by elaborate rock-cut replicas of architectural elements. This phenomenon predated rock-cut architecture by several millennia

cave environments have been used. The Hypogeum is no exception to this general rule. Nevertheless, the manner in which light and darkness were exploited within the Hypogeum emphasizes the simple yet special techniques used within the monument. A number of features suggest that, rather than being a hindrance, the dark environment of the Hypogeum's interior could be put to good use by using the little available light in a thoughtful manner. For instance, a series of upright megaliths placed strategically in the transitory space leading down to the Middle Level may have served to filter and direct natural sunlight. Whether this light would have been able to penetrate right into the innermost chambers is a matter of debate. However, the raised doorway linking the Main Chamber with the Holy of Holies does appear to have been carved precisely with such an intention in mind. Indeed, the doorway provides a visual link between the interior of the Holy of Holies, the Main Chamber, the Intermediate Level, and, from there, the Upper Level. This inter-relationship of spaces along an axis of illumination may have been linked to the significance of possible rites that may have taken place within the Main Chamber and the Holy of Holies, although we cannot now be sure of the nature of such activities.

Finally, the use of natural light seems to have been one of the factors that influenced the manner in which the layout and the use of space within the Hypogeum developed. The area located directly on the main axis of the main entrance received the best possible illumination. Considering that this main axis runs roughly north-west to south-east, natural lighting would have been at its best during the summer months, just before and after the equinox. Summer light would have enabled a more efficient use of daylight hours during the cutting and elaboration of the relief carvings in the Main Chamber and in the Holy of Holies. This first area will be referred to as Zone A. Zone B is the almost-circular chamber that lies adjacent to the Main Chamber. This second zone received less lighting and is likewise not decorated with any relief carvings. The third zone, C, lies perpendicular to the main axis of the Middle Level. It therefore receives much less light than the other two zones. To compensate, the prehistoric craftsmen carved the main chamber in this zone to a roughly rectangular plan, thus securing the best possible penetration of natural light.

Zone A is recognizable as an important focal space. The zone is distinguished by two chambers cut in close physical succession along the main axis of the Hypogeum. Both chambers are decorated with elaborate relief carvings that emulate architectural elements. At first sight, the features appear to be exact replicas of temple architectural elements. Yet on closer inspection, a number of differences are immediately noticeable. The embellishment in the main chamber consists largely in a simple composition of vertical and horizontal curves. The vertical curves are cut to a symmetrical arrangement on either side of the raised doorway that leads into the Holy of Holies. The ceiling of the chamber is also fashioned in such a manner as to replicate, in part, the idea of corbelled roofing. This arrangement

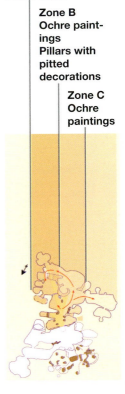

Zone A
Architectural replicas
Ochre wash

Zone B
Ochre paint-ings
Pillars with pitted decorations

Zone C
Ochre paintings

Opposite: **A line of vision linking the beautifully carved main chamber with the innermost 'Holy of Holies', was created by a port entrance. The exquisite finish of the carvings reflect accomplished craftsmanship. Metal tools are not known from Late Neolithic Malta**

Above: The two windows lining the Main Chamber in Zone A with the painted chamber of Zone B. The windows provided additional light. In the Main Chamber the windows were embellished with trilithons and separated by an ochre painted chequered design

Right: The beautifully carved screen which separates the 'Holy of Holies' from the Main Chamber

Opposite: The recesses in the north-east wall of the Main Chamber

is then mirrored on the ground by an almost complete circular perimeter that defines the floor space of the chamber. The entire composition is first viewed through a large circular opening that visitors encounter when standing in the interior lobby of the Hypogeum. The effect is similar to that often experienced in a modern-day camera fish-eye lens only, in the case of the Hypogeum, the illusion was achieved by a thoughtful arrangement of relief carvings. This

play of vertical and horizontal curves captures the essential elements of the aesthetics of Maltese prehistoric art. Curvilinear forms define much of the artistic creations of the time, be they carved spirals, animal representations, or human figures.

The inner chamber, often referred to as the Holy of Holies, is reached rather more easily through the round chamber in Zone B rather than through the Main Chamber. Like the Main Chamber, the Holy of Holies appears to have been accorded a significant status. However, there are a number of important differences. The chamber is marked by a contrast between its interior and exterior. While the exterior is a highly-accomplished masterpiece in relief carving, the interior is almost devoid of embellishments and is rather rough in overall finishes. The exterior is

Top: The Holy of Holies

Above: The two tethering holes were still covered with plugs at the time of excavations

Opposite: The main entrance in the central screen of the Main Chamber

eye-catching enough to become one of Malta's cultural icons. Its composition follows even more closely the elements of a temple façade, but not without some significant differences. For instance, the space just in font of the Holy of Holies recalls a temple's internal apse, rather than an external space that is often found in front of temples. Indeed, the ceiling in this 'intermediate' ante-space even follows the principles of corbelling in a more pronounced manner than in the case of the Main Chamber. The overall effect is the reverse of what one experiences in a temple – an interior apse with a partially corbelled roofing, decorated with an external façade. As in the case of many of the temples, the façade comes equipped with two 'rope holes', which are usually found to the left of a temple's main entrance.

The roughly-finished interior of the chamber is still a subject of debate. What was this interior originally used for? Why does the doorway have tie-holes on the inside only? Was it meant to be closed off from within and isolate its occupants? Or were these features a later addition linked to a ritual? Why does the interior give the impression that it was left in an unfinished state? Indeed the interior of the chamber does not do justice to the splendid façade of the Holy of Holies. Why is there such a contrast?

Such questions shall remain a matter of debate. In the first place, the interior of the Holy of Holies appears to have evolved through a number of changes. The present state of the chamber represents its last transformation. Originally, the chamber comprised an altar consisting of a high ridge that was

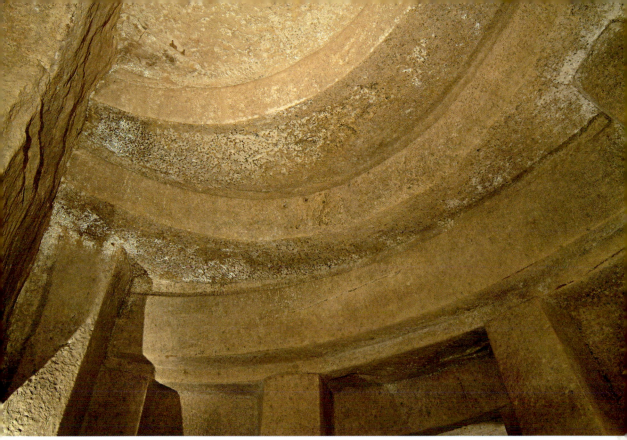

flanked by two pillars. The floor of the chamber is sunk in order to provide comfortable standing room for occupants, or else, as in other chambers within the Hypogeum, to provide a sunken perimeter to hold soil and burials. The altar thus consisted of a raised shelf or platform that was partly hollowed out of the back wall of the chamber. At some point during prehistory, the niche was modified. The left-hand pillar was partly removed and the back wall may have been cut away to its present dimensions. The surface of the ledge is marked by a circular hollow, cut to a depth of about 30 cm. The second interesting feature is found immediately above this hollow. The ceiling rock was at some point cut in such a way as to form a vertical protrusion through which a hole was cut. Clearly, this tie-hole may have been intended to carry an

object above the circular hollow on the ledge. Was such an object meant to be seen from outside?

The relief carvings of the Middle Level provide an insight into the way that the inhabitants of prehistoric Malta may have conceptualized some aspects of the afterlife. It is indeed commonplace throughout world archaeology for scholars to discover that expressions of life after death emulate life itself. Several ancient civilizations are renowned for their elaborate burial rites which, apart from including monuments, comprise a complex repertoire of objects and personal possessions. In some cases, the afterlife was thought of as being a journey, which among many stages included a presence in an 'underworld'. Indeed, the notion of the underworld became itself a euphemism or a metaphor that helped communities come to terms

Above: **The carved ceiling, representing partial corbelling, in the lobby in front of the 'Holy of Holies'**

Opposite: **The doorway in the central rock-cut screen of the Main Chamber, provides a visual line from the 'Holy of Holies' to the external areas lying beyond this innermost sanctury**

Within, the 'Holy of Holies' gives the impression that the chamber had been modified

The view of the niches of the Main Chamber as seen from the decorated room in Zone B

through familiar environments as well as familiar cultural icons. The megalithic temples would have provided familiar reference points in a landscape that was also very familiar. For the inhabitants of the Maltese islands, cemeteries such as the Hypogeum may have served to combine the complexities of an underworld and an afterlife with the realities of everyday life, through a visual metaphor.

To the right of Zone A, lies Zone B. This space comprises a single chamber, which at first sight appears to be not as elaborate as the chambers of Zone A. The chamber is roughly circular in plan. Its purpose may have been different from that attributed to other parts of the Hypogeum. Among other functions, the chamber also doubled up as a passage-way leading to the Holy of Holies and the entrance to the Lower Level. The circular character of the chamber is given mainly by the right-hand wall, which also defines the main segment

with loss. In many civilizations, the underworld becomes the subject of myths, an equally effective narration for mediating the past with social realities. Metaphors can, of course, take a number of forms. Our concern, in this case, is the visual metaphor that is so common in public monuments. At the Hypogeum, the use of architectural idioms may have provided a familiar language that communities could understand. The dead may have warranted a rite of passage that could somehow be mediated

of the chamber's space. This wall arches upwards and joins up with the ceiling to form a dome-like profile for the entire chamber. All around, to a height of about a metre from the chamber's floor, the wall was not refined and tidied of prehistoric drill holes and rock-cutting scars. Soil marks suggest that this level was covered over by earth and was, therefore, not visible. Beyond this level, however, the entire 'dome' feature was given a smoother finish, the surface being intended for painting. At least three painted patterns can be identified across the ceiling and wall of the chamber. One pattern comprises a system of polygons. Yet another is made up of spirals. Some polygons were provided with spirals. Finally, a plant-like pattern, a derivative of the classical Maltese spiral, extends across the ceiling towards the polygon and spiral patterns. The patterns now form what appears to be a single composition, although in certain places, they overlap slightly,

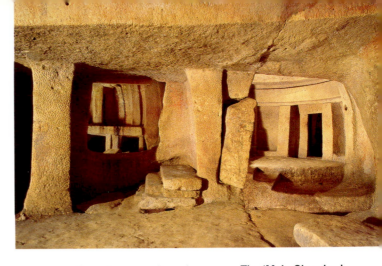

suggesting that they may have been painted at different times. The paintings are rendered in red ochre, a pigment which was widely used during burial rituals.

Directly opposite the painted wall, lies the separating wall that divided Zone B from Zone A. In reality, this separating wall is a structure made up of two main enclosures. The first of these consists of a recess with a deep pit for a floor. The pit is almost 2 m deep and cut to a bell-shape. The entrance to this enclosure is slightly raised, with a groove cut

The 'Main Chamber' and the 'Holy of Holies' in Zone A as seen from the Main Chamber in Zone B

The ochre spiral design on the ceiling of the Decorated Room

across to hold a slab that may have been intended to separate the pit from the main chamber of Zone B. It was in this pit enclosure that the renowned figure of the 'sleeping lady' was discovered. The neighbouring enclosure consists of a rectangular space, with a series of slabs for a floor. These slabs cover the mouth of a deep cavity that leads down into the lower level of the Hypogeum. This cavity may have originally served as either the entrance to the Lower Level or else as an access point from which debris could be hauled up during the expansion of the lower storey. Seen from Zone B, the enclosure still captures some of its original significance. A striking feature of the enclosure is a pit-decorated pillar arrangement which is very similar to the pillar niche found at Lower Mnajdra. The monumental arrangement may have indeed served to highlight the entrance to the Lower Level.

To the right of Zones A and B lies the third Zone, C, which comprises a main rectangular chamber from which two side chambers can be accessed. The chamber's floor is sunk to a depth of about a metre. As in other places within the Hypogeum, soil marks suggest that the chamber had once been partly filled with soil. This may have been uneven in depth, but in some places it may have reached the level of the lobby floor. The ceiling of the chamber is

Opposite: **The deep pit, in Zone B**

Below: **The stair-like slabs are actually the roof of the stairs leading to the Lower Level**

Bottom: **Red ochre spiral design in Zone C**

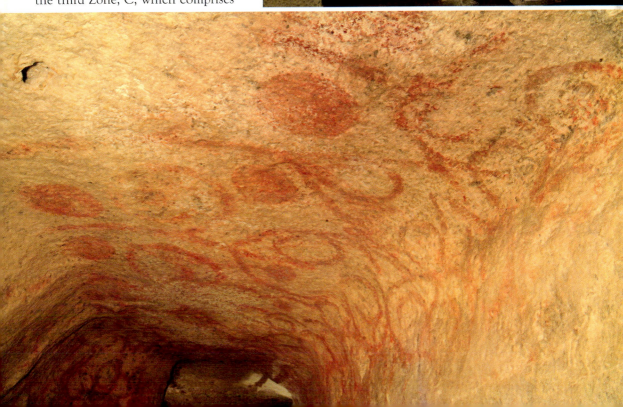

Three red ochre disks embellished a prominent niche in Zone C. Modern myth would have us believe that the niche was imbued with special acoustic qualities that were once used by an oracle

decorated with red ochre paintings of spirals and related motifs. The designs are more organic and less geometric than the ones noted in the main chamber of Zone B. Notably absent are the polygon forms. Immediately to the left of the entrance lies a curvilinear hollow. This feature is crudely finished, probably the result of an unfinished effort to cut a side chamber. The back wall of the hollow is pierced by two holes that connect this feature with chamber 21. Further along the left wall of the main chamber of Zone C is the entrance to a side chamber. This entrance is almost a square in form and, interestingly enough, now located at about .85 cm above the floor. A closer examination of the soil marks on the wall of the main chamber shows that these reached the exact height of the square entrance. This suggests that this side chamber may have been cut following the introduction of soil into Zone C. Further along lies a niche that was originally painted with red ochre designs. Some of these are still visible. This niche may have once held an object of some significance, possibly a statuette or a figurine. On the right-hand wall of the main chamber of Zone C, a small access hole leads to a largish side chamber. The plan of this chamber is somewhat irregular, but finely carved. An interesting feature is the ceiling of the room, which slopes upwards to a height of almost 3 m away from the entrance. Opposite the entrance is a small circular room measuring about a metre in diameter.

The Lower Level is accessed through an entrance that is located in front of the 'Holy of Holies' in Zone A. This entrance is highlighted

by a trilithon which is built into a corresponding hollow. Unlike most of the architectural features found within the Hypogeum, the trilithon is not cut from the live rock. The monumental entrance leads to a series of steps that lead down to a transitory space, chamber 28. The last of these steps is supported by two upright megaliths. These megaliths are 2 m high and rest immediately on the floor of chamber 28. The depth at which the floor of this chamber is found, provides a dramatic drop from the floor of the Middle Level. The flight of steps leading down to the Lower Level now appear to end abruptly in mid-air. As in several other chambers in the Hypogeum, the inexplicable floor depth of this transitory space may have been intended to contain a substantial soil deposit. In fact, during the excavation of the monument, Zammit

The Lower Level is reached from a flight of steps. The last of these, the seventh, is supported by two upright megaliths

Overleaf: A carved trilithon marks the entrance to the Lower Level

Below: A magnificent 'keystone' cut out and inserted into a special hollow above the seven steps leading to the Lower Level

The flight of steps leading to the Lower Level known as 'the Seven Uneven Steps'

A 275° view of the Lower Level chambers

noted that chamber 28 was found to contain debris that provided flooring and access into the chambers of the Lower Level.

The Lower Level chambers are accessible through a rock-cut trilithon. This imposing entrance reflects the same standard of craftsmanship that was employed in the Middle Level. The trilithon leads to an arrangement of spaces that are separated by narrow walls. These walls rise to a height of just under 2 m above the floor of the

The inner chambers

The supports under the stairs

The pilaster supporting the Holy of Holies

The back of the entrance trilithon to the Lower Level

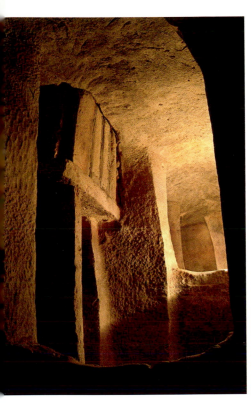

Lower Level, giving the entire complex of chambers an unusual character. As in the case of chamber 28, the arrangement of the Lower Level now gives a misleading impression. Once again, the high walls may have been originally intended to contain substantial amounts of soil and debris, but Zammit's excavation notes discount this in the case of the Lower Level chambers.

Left: **The supports of the seven steps on the trilithon in the Lower Level**

Above: **The floor of the deepest cavity (on the left) reaches a depth of 10.6 metres below ground**

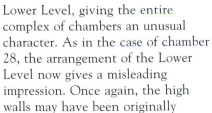

The walls of the Lower Level have a spread of red ochre in some places

Lower Level chamber with the rock partitions

Another pilaster supporting the Holy of Holies

Middle Level

25

24

23

20

Zone B

18

26

22

19

Zone A

21

27   28   29

Zone C

16

17

15

13   14

12

Upper Level

9   6

7

8

10

11

Recent excavations
now under modern
wall and street

5

metres
0 1 2 3 4 5

THE ITINERARY

(1) Exhibition area
The modest display provides a brief overview of the archaeology of the Hypogeum. The Hypogeum is explained in the broader context of the *temple period* (4000-2500 BC), and the relationship that the monument had with megalithic buildings of the time. Highlights of the display include a life-size copy of the *Sleeping Lady*, information concerning the builders of the magnificent temples, prehistoric burial rituals and grave art, as well as information regarding pioneers of Maltese archaeology.
A selection of artefacts originally found at the Hypogeum provides a glimpse into the variety of votive offerings that accompanied the dead. A central exhibition panel shows drawn plans of the different levels of the Hypogeum.

(2) Audiovisual presentation
The audio-visual show presents a brief documentary on the importance and significance of the Hal Saflieni Hypogeum. A renowned World Heritage Site, the Hypogeum was discovered in 1902, during housing projects. The documentary charts the different passageways, chambers and niches that make up the subterranean monument. In addition, it provides a number of theories on how the cemetery may have been used, and how it once formed part of a wider world in which temples and megalithic buildings shaped everyday life in the Maltese islands.

UPPER LEVEL

(3) On entering the protected area, visitors step onto a modern walkway. The walkway, which is totally reversible and designed to provide a first level of protection for the monument, leads visitors to all the accessible areas of the monument. Standing at the uppermost point of the walkway, visitors can get a bird's eye view of the Upper Level. The level had been bridged over by foundation walls on which early nineteenth century houses rested. In a few places, foundation trenches have scarred the prehistoric surface of the Upper Level.

(4) Moving along the modern walkway, visitors walk past a group of small megaliths. These stones may have once formed part of a monument that may have extended on to the surface area of the Hypogeum.

(5) The walkway directs visitors on to the main axis of the Upper Level. The floor of the Upper Level stands at about 2 metres below the current street level. The floor is the bottom of a large hollow that was fashioned out of the promontory on which the Hypogeum is located. The natural side of the promontory was cut away during prehistory so that access to the Hypogeum could be facilitated. The profile of this access point can still be made out under the modern wall which lies directly opposite the entrance to the Middle Level.

Standing in the middle of the Upper Level, one notes a number of chambers cut into the rock walls. Three roughly cut chambers, with low headroom, stand to the right of the main axis **(7)**. A monumental trilithon lies to a left of the main axis. **(8)** The trilithon may have once formed part of a more extensive structure, which has now disappeared. Beyond the trilithon lies a group of chambers **(9)** and **(10)** that lead to cistern **(11)**. Chamber **(10)**, still retains a substantial deposit of earth and human remains. The deposit was left in situ by Sir Temi Zammit and is now being preserved for future generations of researchers. The cistern reaches a depth of almost 8 meters.

(12) Before entering the underground chambers, look under the left hand side of the platform and see an opening in the roof of a chamber with walls cut perfectly perpendicular (photo 12A). On the right hand side, just next to the platform are two 'tethering' holes, such holes are found near the entrance of the above ground temples (photo 12B). Here some of the original bones and soil can be seen (photo 12C). A perfect circle cut in the rock covers a hole in the ground (photo 12D).

MIDDLE LEVEL

An intermediate space **(13)** links the Upper with the Middle level. To the left of the walkway, in chamber **(14)**, visitors can still see an excavation spoil heap left behind from Magri's and Zammit's campaigns. The complex arrangements of chambers and standing stones gives a flavour of what lies in the interior areas of the Middle Level. Of particular interest are the standing stones. Some scholars believe that these may have originally been set up to define a common passage way and to filter natural light entering the level's interior. Among the more interesting features of this intermediate space is a chamber that is entered through a circular hole in the

ground **(15)**. Above this chamber, visitors can still see modern arches that once supported house foundations.

From the intermediate space, visitors immediately descend into the lobby area **(16)** of the Middle Level proper. To the right, stands a monumental trilithon **(17)**. Standing in the 'lobby area', take time to note the three zones that form the Middle Level. The Zones, A, B and C, received varying levels of light. The spaces of these three zones are characterised by contrasting plans and decorations. Notice the unfinished state of the lobby area. In several places, drill holes used to quarry away the rock as the Hypogeum was being formed. The holes are what now remains of that age-old practice of drill and lever method of rock cutting.

Zone A is the most complex part of the Hypogeum. The zone comprises two areas, the Main Chamber followed by the 'Holy of Holies'. The main chamber is distinguished by rock-cut replicas of a temple facade **(18)**. To the left of the chamber a number of niches are cut into the wall **(19)**. The right-hand wall is characterized by two windows that link this area with Zone B **(20)**. The entire chamber is decorated by an eye-catching arrangement of vertical and horizontal curves. From the lobby area, the main Chamber is viewed through a large round opening. Together, these curves create a visual play on the viewer, the effect being very similar to that of 'fish eye' camera lens. Recent conservation measures have exposed areas of colour, suggesting that the chamber may have once been painted red. Other designs are certainly present: a chequered decoration can still be seen in between the two windows in wall **(20)**.

Zone B is characterized by a large elliptical chamber, with two cavities cut into the ground. One of these features, pit **(21)**, is thought to be the final resting place of the 'Sleeping Lady'. The pit was finished to a high standard of craftsmanship. This, together with the discovery of the 'Sleeping Lady', suggests that the pit may have once

served as a repository of votive offerings. Along side this pit lies a shaft **(22)** which leads to the Lower Level. The shaft was cut in between two decorated pillars of the type found in temples and is covered by slabs. The ceiling of the chamber **(23)** is decorated by a series of paintings. The paintings, made with red ochre, comprise a series of spirals, polygons and a plant-like design which is very much akin to the spiral motif.

This chamber, often referred to as the 'Holy of Holies', is one of Malta's more iconic symbols. The space comprises a beautifully carved replica of a temple facade **(24)**, complete with typical tethering holes cut in front, but slightly to the left of the chamber's entrance. The space is characterised by a replica of a partially corbelled ceiling **(A)**. Within, the chamber is roughly finished. The floor is sunk to a lower depth than that of the external standing floor, thus affording ample standing space. At the back of the chamber stands a table ledge **(25)**, with a shallow round hollow cut into its surface. Above this is a small rock outcrop which was pierced in order to allow an object to be hung. Opposite the 'Holy of Holies' lie a monumental entrance and seven steps **(26)** that lead down to the Lower Level.

Zone C consists primarily of a long chamber, two side chambers and a niche. The ceiling of the main chamber is decorated with red ochre spiral paintings **(27)**. These are more organic in form and are not enclosed in polygons as in the case of the spirals in Zone B. Soil marks still appearing on the walls **(28)** suggest that the chamber was once full of earth. The surface of the soil deposit would have provided a standing floor that would have been at a level with the standing floors of space **(16)**. A modern myth of oracle acoustics has developed around the niche at **(29)**. The niche, which is decorated with red ochre discs, has been used as an 'echo sounder' by hundreds of visitors, in the belief that this hollow once served as a form of primitive amplifier by an oracle. Modern hand marks left by visitors are still visible.

FURTHER READING

A number of studies help to place the Hypogeum in a wider context. Among the standard texts, those by Sir Themistocles Zammit, John D. Evans, and David Trump remain essential publications. Zammit's *The Ħal Saflieni Prehistoric Hypogeum* (1910) and *The Ħal SaflieniHypogeum* (1925), capture the spirit of the age of discovery. The first work describes the work that had been undertaken at the Hypogeum by 1910. This did not include the excavation of the Upper Level, which work is reported in full in the 1925 version of the original publication. Read together, the two works provide a useful guide to dating and understanding the monument. J.D. Evans' *The Prehistoric Antiquities of the Maltese Islands* (London, 1971) provides a detailed survey of standard sources on Maltese archaeology as well as a detailed description of the monument. The Evans survey included an updated mapping of all the chambers of the Hypogeum. This mapping is still a standard reference point for discussing the monument. David Trump provides important dating information in *Skorba* (Oxford, 1966). The more recent developments at the Hypogeum are covered in Anthony Pace's *The Ħal Saflieni Hypogeum 4000 BC -2000 AD* (2000) which provides a broad archaeological context for understanding the Hypogeum, the recent excavations at the site as well as useful information regarding the conservation of the monument.